MW01033460

The Sabbath
Entering God's Rest

Barry & Steffi Rubin

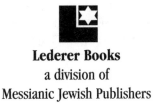

Lederer Books
a division of
Messianic Jewish Publishers

Also by the same authors . . .
You Bring the Bagels, I'll Bring the Gospel:
        Sharing the Messiah with Your Jewish Neighbor (Barry Rubin)
Dedicate and Celebrate:
        A Messianic Jewish Guide to Hanukkah (Barry and Steffi Rubin)
It is Good! Growing Up in a Messianic Jewish Family (Steffi Rubin)
The Messianic Passover Haggadah (Barry Rubin)
The Messianic Passover Seder Preparation Guide (Barry and Steffi Rubin)

Unless otherwise indicated, all Scripture quotations are taken from the
Complete Jewish Bible, Copyright © 1998 by David H. Stern, published by Jewish
New Testament Publications, Inc.

Printed in the United States of America
Cover by Now You See it! graphics

05 04 03 02 01   7 6 5 4 3 2
ISBN 1-880226-74-X

Library of Congress Catalog Control Number: 99229097

Lederer Books
a division of
Messianic Jewish Publishers
6204 Park Heights Ave.
Baltimore, Maryland 21215
(410) 358-6471

Distributed by
Messianic Jewish Resources International
Individual order line: (800) 410-7367
Trade order line: (800) 773-MJRI (6574)
E-mail: lederer@messianicjewish.net
Website: www.messianicjewish.net

Part 1

Should the Sabbath be Kept?

Barry (Baruch) Rubin

Introduction

*W*ell-known author Norman Mailer once observed that New York City would benefit from having all the electricity turned off for one day a week. People could stop their frantic activities and reflect a bit. Mailer understood the importance of *Shabbat*, the Sabbath, even though it's doubtful he was thinking of a day for worship.

Shabbat is meaningful to both Jews and Christians. A Jewish tradition states that when all Israel—as a nation—keeps the Sabbath, the Messiah will come. Whether or not the rabbis who postulated this position literally believed it, it demonstrates how important they deemed *Shabbat* to be.

Another way of expressing the special nature of this day is the traditional Jewish saying: "A precious jewel have I in my possession, which I wish to give to Israel, and Sabbath is its name." Another viewpoint is that "the Sabbaths were given to Israel in order that they might study *Torah*." The widely-read author, Herman Wouk, said in *This is My God*, "The Sabbath is the usual breaking off point from tradition, and also the point at which many Jews rejoin Judaism" (p. 61). Keeping the Sabbath holy was an "acid test" of who was an observant Jew.

The Sabbath has meant something to Christians, as well. The New Testament records many discussions about this day. Moreover, the Sabbath day is a symbol of eternity. In post-biblical times, the Catholic Church even went so far as to *insist* on its observance, but on Sunday, the first day of the week. Because of the importance of *Shabbat* to the Jewish people, this change of day by the Catholic Church, as much as anything else, made "Christianity" anathema to Jews. Much controversy revolves around *Shabbat*.

There are many books on the Sabbath. Lederer/Messianic Jewish Publishers—the organization that I direct—published one called *Shabbat: Celebrating the Sabbath the Messianic Jewish Way*. Because I wanted to address some of the controversial aspects surrounding the Sabbath, as well as offer a complete handbook for keeping the Sabbath, I decided to write a new book on the subject of *Shabbat*.

Previously, my theological view, like that of many believers, didn't allow much room for a high position on the Sabbath. I intuited that it was probably a good idea to have a day of rest, one in seven. But it didn't really matter much to me. I was confused as to what Messiah's statement, "I have come to fulfill the Law," meant as it related to *Shabbat*. Back then, I believed that his "fulfilling the Law" meant I was free from the need to follow the Law. Discovering that the expression "fulfill" was a Hebrew idiom meaning "to interpret correctly" helped me to understand what Yeshua meant. "I have come to interpret the *Torah* correctly, not incorrectly (i.e., 'to abolish the Law')."

Furthermore, the day on which to take this day of rest didn't matter to me, either. I was pastoring the oldest "Messianic congregation" in the country. Having been influenced by the Presbyterians, who began it in the early 1900s, the congregation observed Sunday as their day of worship. At first, this was fine with me.

However, my wife, along with my two daughters, desired to keep a more Sabbath-observant home, and began instituting certain Sabbath practices. (She will share some of these in this book.) Because of the change in our home, as well as my own re-examination of certain theological presuppositions I had always held, I began to study the Scriptures to understand more about the Sabbath. The result of my research, coupled with my "ladies'" instinctive change, led to my change of views.

As you read this book, I hope you will consider not only the ways you can enjoy this special day, but understand its background as well. I believe you will be blessed by learning more about the Sabbath—its Scriptural basis and its special practices—and how it has been misunderstood.

As we Jews say when we begin our Sabbath observance, "*Shabbat shalom*." May you have a Sabbath of peace . . . even into eternity.

What is the Sabbath?

The word *Shabbat*, or Sabbath, primarily means "to cease or desist." In relation to God, it pertains to the Creation.

> On the seventh day God was finished with his work which he had made, so he rested on the seventh day. . . . God blessed the seventh day and separated it as holy (Gen. 2:2–3a).

After six days of work, God had ceased creating and "rested." Was God tired? Of course not. He has unlimited strength. Pertaining to the memorializing of this day, Rabbi Hayim Halevy Donin wrote in *To Be a Jew*,

> . . .what does the *Torah* [Pentateuch] teach us when it says that "God rested"? Is He human that He tires and needs physical rest? It is to teach us that just as God stopped creating physical things on the seventh day, so is man to stop creating on this day. Man is to stop making things, to stop manipulating nature. . . . By desisting from all such labors, we not only acknowledge the existence of a Creator, but also emulate the Divine example (p. 65).

God made this day holy, or "set apart." It's truly a day on which we can spend twenty-four uninterrupted hours focusing on the Lord. It's a time when we can cease our busy-ness and examine the eternal aspects of life. If we are to follow him, we should treat this day in a special way. It was created for us.

When is the Sabbath?

It's one thing to understand the principle of ceasing from creating, but another to decide when this day should be observed. God began teaching this to his people even before the Sabbath laws were given. Recorded in the sixteenth chapter of Exodus, in response to the "grumblings of the people of Isra'el,"

> *Adonai* said to Moshe, "Here, I will cause bread to rain down from heaven for you. The people are to go out and gather a day's ration every day. By this I will test whether they will observe my *Torah* or not. On the sixth day, when they prepare what they have brought in, it will turn out to be twice as much as they gather on the other days" (Exod. 16:4–5).

Not only was this a clarification of which day the Sabbath was to be observed, it was also an admission that God was testing his people—using Sabbath observance—to see if they would follow the *Torah*. Then, in the Ten Commandments, the Sabbath was codified:

> Remember the day, *Shabbat*, to set it apart for God. You have six days to labor and do all your work, but the seventh day is a *Shabbat* for ADONAI your God. On it, you are not to do any kind of work. . . . For in six days ADONAI made heaven and earth, the sea and everything in them; but on the seventh day he rested. This is why ADONAI blessed the day, *Shabbat*, and separated it for himself (Exod. 20:8–11).

Based on the fourth commandment, there is no doubt that the Sabbath, when initially instituted, was the seventh day. (I will address the "Christian" first day of the week Sabbath later.) God wanted humanity to remember his Creation on the day he rested. By observing it then, people would identify with God's ceasing work on the Creation. This gift was given in part so that humanity would remember who the Creator was . . . and rest in him.

But when does the seventh day begin? Midnight on Friday? Six in the morning on Saturday? When?

The answer is that it begins just after sundown on the sixth day. In other words, the seventh-day *Shabbat* begins on Friday evening. This conclusion was reached after considering the verses in the Creation account, where it is written, "So there was evening, and there was morning, one day" (Gen. 1:5b). This statement appears again after each of the six days of creation. Thus, the nation of Israel has always observed its holy days (including *Shabbat*) from sundown on one day to sundown the following day. This fact will clarify some centuries-old Christian misconceptions that I will discuss later.

Whom is the Sabbath For?

In the beginning, God designed *Shabbat* as a reminder that he rested on the seventh day, and as a day for us to spend with him. In time, another important meaning was revealed:

> You are to observe my *Shabbat*s; for this is a sign between me and you through all your generations; so that you will know that I am ADONAI, who sets you

apart for me. Therefore you are to keep my *Shabbat*, because it is set apart for you. The people of Isra'el are to keep the *Shabbat*, to observe *Shabbat* through all their generations as a perpetual covenant. It is a sign between me and the people of Isra'el forever; for in six days A*DONAI* made heaven and earth, but on the seventh day he stopped working and rested (Exod. 31:13–17).

This special day was a permanent sign signifying that God "set apart," that is, made holy, the nation of Israel. It reminded the nation of her unique calling and responsibility. That is why it was to be taken so seriously:

Everyone who treats it [the Sabbath] as ordinary must be put to death; for whoever does any work on it is to be cut off from his people. On six days work will get done; but the seventh day is *Shabbat*, for complete rest, set apart for A*DONAI*. Whoever does any work on the day of *Shabbat* must be put to death (Exod. 31:14b–15).

This ultimate penalty ensured that God's people would obey this commandment. They would receive the blessing of rest, remember the Creation, and recall the covenant God made with them.

The words of Isaiah affirm this truth: "Happy is the person who does this, anyone who grasps it firmly, who keeps *Shabbat* and does not profane it, and keeps himself from doing any evil" (Isa. 56:2).

God desired to bless his people through this holy day. But it was not given just to the Jewish people; it was given, too, to reveal insight into eternal truths to *all* humanity:

And the foreigners who join themselves to A*DONAI* to serve him, to love the name of A*DONAI*, and to be his workers, all who keep *Shabbat* and do not profane it . . . I will bring them to my holy mountain and make them joyful in my house of prayer (Isa. 56:6–7a).

In fact, Isaiah also shares that in the days of the new heavens and the new earth, ". . . every week on *Shabbat*, everyone living will come to worship in my presence, says A*DONAI*" (Isa. 66:23); a Sabbath rest will be the reward for all who enter eternity with God. Thus, by observing *Shabbat* now, we prepare for eternity.

The Sabbath is for all mankind—given before the Ten Commandments were issued, guarded by Israel for centuries, and guaranteed in eternity to all who trust the Lord.

Did Yeshua the Messiah Cancel Sabbath-Keeping?

The fact that this is a real question in the minds of many demonstrates that, because of historical and theological error, much misunderstanding surrounds *Shabbat.* There was confusion even in Messiah's time. How to keep this day holy was often on the minds of the Jewish people then. That's why Yeshua was asked questions about the Sabbath practices of his followers. Misinterpretation of his responses has contributed to Christians' confusion about this day.

Two examples of such questions and answers are recorded in Matthew 12:1–13, a confrontation between Yeshua and some Pharisees. They questioned Messiah on two issues: whether it was acceptable for his *talmidim* (disciples) to pick grain on the Sabbath (Matt. 12:1–2), and whether it was acceptable to heal on this holy day (Matt. 12:10). Yeshua's responses clarified and restored the original intent of keeping the Sabbath holy, but his words have been misunderstood by many.

By this time in Jewish history, 39 *m'la'khot* (works) were prohibited on *Shabbat.* These restrictions were based on the work performed in the construction of the Tabernacle. The rabbis reasoned that since work on the Tabernacle was to cease on *Shabbat,* the activities associated with its construction were therefore also not acceptable for *Shabbat.*

Included in this list (found in *Mishnah Shabbat* 7:2) was "reaping." To the Pharisees, Yeshua's *talmidim* were reaping. They were picking grain as they walked through the fields; this conformed to a rabbinical definition of reaping. In the parallel passage to the Matthew 12 portion, Luke reports that the disciples had rubbed the heads of the grains together (6:1). This was defined as "threshing," also unlawful according to rabbinical interpretation of the Sabbath rules (*Talmud Shabbat* 73a–75b).

It's not surprising that the Pharisees wanted to know why Yeshua's *talmidim* were doing this. The Pharisees were charged with the responsibility of protecting the people from those who would teach against the Law of Moses. Yeshua's response, however, showed them that his *talmidim* were actually following the Law.

In answer to the first question, then, Yeshua focused attention on King David and the *cohanim* (priests). Both examples were offered to prove that, to God, the intent of the heart is more important than the observance of rules and regulations.

Yeshua addressed the second question, pertaining to healing on the Sabbath, in a similar way. He got the *P'rushim* (Pharisees) to look at their own interpretation of their Sabbath laws, by asking,

If you have a sheep that falls into a pit on *Shabbat*, which of you won't take hold of it and lift it out? How much more valuable is a man than a sheep! Therefore, what is permitted on *Shabbat* is to do good (Matt. 12:11–12).

Nowadays, perhaps in part because of Yeshua's teaching, Jewish people would not question the act of saving a life on the Sabbath. In fact, many Jews held this opinion even at the time of Yeshua.

To conclude his teaching on *Shabbat*, the Messiah stated that this unique day "was made for mankind, not mankind for the *Shabbat*" (Mark 2:27). He was consistent with the Jewish tradition which stated, "the Sabbath was given over to man and not man to the Sabbath" (*Mekhilta, Ki Tissa*:5). Although it had special meaning to the nation of Israel, it was made for all humanity as a day on which "to do good."

Sadly, because of a lack of understanding about Jewish life in the second-Temple period, many have misunderstood Yeshua's teaching. He was not teaching disregard for *Torah*; rather, he was teaching the true meaning of what the *Torah* taught about *Shabbat*.

Yeshua affirmed the keeping of *Shabbat*; he desired that his people get past the traditions that had obscured the true meaning of *Shabbat*. He wanted them to experience the blessing of rest, the remembrance of the Creation, the recollection of the covenant God had made with Israel, and the realization that *Shabbat* was a picture of eternity—one that mankind could enjoy in the present age.

Nowhere did Yeshua teach that the Sabbath could be broken. In fact, he always went to synagogue on *Shabbat*. Yet he did teach that, for good reason, some traditions could be bypassed, and that the hierarchy of Law should be considered in making decisions. (This was demonstrated in the case of the showbread that David's men—not priests—ate when they were famished, and in the fact that the priests "worked" on *Shabbat*.)

In the entire *B'rit Chadashah* (New Covenant), there is not one reference to the believers (nearly all Jewish) violating *Shabbat*. Yeshua loved the Sabbath. Rabbi Sha'ul (the apostle Paul), on his missionary journeys, always went to synagogue on this holy day, not for evangelism, but for worship. The New Testament repeatedly states that he went "as his custom was." He was an Orthodox Jew. Other apostles, too, worshipped on *Shabbat*. Nowhere does the *B'rit Chadashah* teach against obtaining the blessing of *Shabbat*.

Why Don't Christians Keep the Sabbath Day Holy?

To be sure, Christians, for the most part, believe they are keeping the Sabbath by having church services on Sunday. Often we are told that this is done to follow one of the Ten Commandments. We affirm and applaud this.

But you might be asking yourself, "If the New Testament teaches Sabbath observance, that is, making the seventh day of the week special, how is it that Christians worship on Sunday, not the seventh day?

First, we want to make it clear that any day of the week is a good day on which to worship God. If people want to gather on Tuesday at 2:38 P.M. to have a worship service, that's fine. God will be pleased. But what I don't think pleases him is that many of his people—Christians—believe that the Sabbath moved from the seventh day to the first day of the week.

Nowhere in Scripture is Israel (or anyone else) instructed to have a holy convocation on the first day of the week. The holy convocation of Israel was to be on the Sabbath, the seventh day. According to Robert Odom in *Sabbath and Sunday in Early Christianity*,

> The New Testament writings say nothing about the first day of the week being divinely blessed or set apart as holy to be observed. . . . They do not speak of it as a sacred day of rest, nor do they forbid secular work on it.

If one looks honestly at the New Testament, one sees, as did Dr. Lyman Abbot, an American Congregationalist, that "The current notion that Christ and His apostles authoritatively substituted the first day for the Seventh, is absolutely without any authority in the New Testament" ("Christian Union," June 26, 1890). And as James Cardinal Gibbons, a Catholic theologian, declared in *The Faith of Our Fathers*, "You may read the Bible from Genesis to Revelation, and you will not find a single line authorizing the sanctification of Sunday. The Scriptures enforce the religious observance of Saturday, a day which we never sanctify."

Why then do most Christian churches convocate on Sunday?

Some teach that Paul gathered with his friends on the first day of the week to break bread, and that this was the reason the Church changed the Sabbath day from the seventh to the first day of the week. Apart from the danger of creating a doctrine from a practice, their facts are simply wrong.

They assume Paul gathered with his friends on Sunday morning, when church was held. But that's reading back into the text. Acts 20:7 does indicate that they met on the "first day of the week"; however, in biblical times (and to this day), the "first day of the week" starts on Saturday night, after the Sabbath is over. As I stated before, the biblical day begins and ends at sundown.

The apostle to the Gentiles was meeting for *Motza'ey-Shabbat*, the meal after the Sabbath. That explains how he was able to speak until midnight. He didn't begin at 11:00 Sunday morning; he probably began late in the evening on Saturday. He wanted to be with his friends before he left for Assos the next morning (Sunday). Paul, a practicing Pharisee, would not have traveled on *Shabbat*, since that was against the *Torah*. The belief that Paul's "first day of the week" teachings occurred on Sunday morning is one of the errors espoused by some teachers.

According to Rev. P. Geieman, "We observe Sunday instead of Saturday because the Catholic Church, in the Council of Laodicea, transferred the solemnity from Saturday to Sunday" (*Convert's Catechism of Catholic Doctrine*, p. 50. London 1934).

It may be suprising to hear, but Messiah probably did not rise on Sunday morning. The Day of First Fruits (*Yom HaBikkurim*) began immediately after sunset on Saturday evening, after *Shabbat* was over. According to Paul, Messiah was "the firstfruits of the resurrection" (1 Cor. 15:20). Thus, *Yom HaBikkurim* is the most likely time of Yeshua's resurrection. The fact is that the New Testament tells us when the first visitors arrived at his tomb, but is silent about the exact time he rose from the dead.

It's hard for traditional Christians to face the fact that the resurrection may not have occurred on Sunday morning. What does one do about Easter services? Considering that the word Easter derives its name from the pagan goddess of fertility, Ishtar, maybe the entire celebration should be reconsidered! Renaming the resurrection day (*Yom HaBikkurim*) "Easter" may have been an attempt by the early church to connect with the pagan world around it.

Sunrise services, although often worshipful, may have been another attempt to connect with the pagan, sun-worshipping world. The name "Sunday" comes from "sun" day, emphasizing the Sun-god of Roman religion. The church attempted to mix sun-worship with Son-worship. Cute, but problematic. It contributed to the church's changing of the Sabbath from the seventh to the first day of the week.

Some say that Sunday is "the Lord's Day." This is a mistranslation and misapplication of Scripture. Revelation 1:10, often cited to justify another *Shabbat*, mentions the "day of the Lord," not "the Lord's Day." This was a vision given to John about the future. To begin with, it's bad biblical interpretation to decide a doctrine from a vision. Calling Sunday "the Lord's Day" was the idea of Sylvester, Bishop of Rome, who, claiming "apostolic authority," decided to make this change (*Historia Ecclestastica*, M. Ludovicum Lucium, Cent. 4, Cap. 10, pp. 739–740. Edition Basilea, 1624).

Yes, the first day can be a day for worship. No need to change that. But the *seventh* day is the day that God set apart to remember the Creation, to recall the covenant he made with his people, and to experience total rest and reflection upon eternity. Let's not confuse the two days; but let's follow what the Lord said and keep the Sabbath holy unto him.

But What About . . . ?

I want to address a few more fallacies before discussing how to prepare for and enjoy *Shabbat*.

I've heard some theologians say, "Since nine of the Ten Commandments are specifically mentioned in the New Testament, but not the fourth commandment about the Sabbath law, it must mean that God authorized changing the day."

To conclude that because the New Testament does not specifically repeat a commandment means that it was done away with is spurious reasoning. Yeshua observed *Shabbat* every week. Its observance was assumed. Additionally, there are many laws of the Torah that are not restated by the Messiah, for example, the laws of incest. No one would conclude that because this wasn't restated, it is therefore now acceptable to practice this sexual perversion.

No, the fact that the New Testament does not specifically restate the fourth commandment does not mean it therefore became inconsequential.

Sometimes we wonder why the same people who argue that Yeshua's not mentioning one of the Ten Commandments proves that that commandment has been changed are so quick to state that he did mention the other nine. Are they saying Gentile believers are obligated to observe them? Are they saying they are "under the Law"? They might say, "Yes, the moral law." But this is a man-made distinction. The Bible does not set apart the Ten Commandments from the rest of the 613 laws, many of them moral. Why focus on nine and exclude the tenth commandment? What about the other 603 laws?

And finally, some say that since Yeshua didn't say, "Keep the seventh day holy," it's fine to keep another. Again, this is a conclusion based on limited information. How do people know that Yeshua did not say to keep the seventh day holy? We don't have records of every word he spoke. He lived like Sabbath-keeping was important, going to synagogue regularly, first with his father and then on his own. One must wonder why Yeshua, who was the agent of Creation and surely, as one with the Father, participated in the development of the Law, would suddenly change the Sabbath. In our opinion, he did not do this.

If this whole issue sounds confusing, that's because it is—if you don't understand the Jewish background of Scripture. I hope this section has shown you the purpose of the Sabbath—that it was given to mankind as a blessing. It's also helpful to know about some of the confused thinking that has arisen from misinformation pertaining to the day. It is our hope that now you will be more able to receive the very special blessing God has for you when you observe the fourth commandment—*Remember the day, Shabbat, to set it apart for God* (Exod. 20:8).

Part 2

Celebrating Shabbat in Your Home

Steffi (Yaffa) Rubin

Preparation: the Count-down Begins

*I*n the homes of many observant Jews the entire week is considered "preparation" for *Shabbat*. It's like a count-down. Daily tasks are done with an eye toward the Sabbath, God's great reward for a week of work.

As the week winds down and the Sabbath draws near, we shift gears from striving to improve our lot to seeking to enrich our spirit. Keeping in mind the Sabbath goal, we approach daily life with purpose and perspective; with *Shabbat* in sight, we plan ahead to tie up loose ends so that they do not become a distraction to our higher purpose.

The *Talmud* says that he who prepares on Friday will eat on the Sabbath (*Avodah Zarah* 3a). As believers, we know that an eternal Sabbath awaits us—one for which we are advised to be spiritually prepared (Heb. 4:9, 10).

Practically speaking, how do we prepare for the Sabbath during the preceding week? One way is to read the weekly *Torah* portion in preparation for Sabbath services. In synagogues the entire *Torah* ("Pentateuch" or "Five Books of Moses") is divided up into weekly readings to be completed during the course of the year. Each weekly portion is separated into seven segments, or *aliyot*—one for each reader who is called up to the *bema*, the podium on which the *Torah* is placed, during the course of the synagogue service. There is also a very short eighth section that can be added to the end of the seventh. If you begin with the first reading on Saturday afternoon or evening and continue to read one section each day you will have completed the entire portion by Friday evening. Schedules of the weekly *Torah* portions can be found in a traditional *Chumash* (a book containing the Five Books of Moses plus associated portions from the Prophets), available in all Jewish bookstores, and in both *A Messianic Jewish Art Calendar* and the *Complete Jewish Bible*, available through Lederer/Messianic Jewish Resources International (see Bibliography).

Preparation might include purchasing something special early in the week for *erev Shabbat* (Sabbath eve; Friday night)—some family favorite to be served for dinner. (We will elaborate on the subject of food later.) Washing your special *Shabbat* tablecloth (traditionally a white one) and lovingly folding it is also an act of preparation. Giving your children special chores to complete before *Shabbat*— room-cleaning, table-setting, music-selection, dinner-planning or preparation—can impart to them a sense of excitement as *Shabbat* draws near. Purchasing flowers or cutting them from your garden and carefully arranging them on the table adds to the festive mood.

Inviting guests is another way to heighten anticipation. If you ask people in advance, their sense of expectancy will grow, too, with the passing of the days. Think of ways to make *Shabbat* a special time of sharing with them. If you have invited someone from your congregation who is familiar with *Shabbat* observance, you can share some family traditions. If it is someone who has never experienced *Shabbat* before, it can be an enriching time of teaching—through Scripture, example and experience.

We realize that many people work outside the home, making many *Shabbat* preparations difficult; in spite of these difficulties, we encourage you to try, where possible, to work some preparation into your busy schedule. If you are able to work flexible hours, try to arrange to be home well in advance of the approaching sundown. This is not usually a problem during daylight savings time, but in the winter, it can be. Still, if you can, try to arrange to arrive home in time to prepare for the Sabbath. Even if you arrive home with precious little time to spare, try to put away work-related items, newspapers, anything that will remind you of day-to-day life.

Remember, do not become discouraged and "forget the whole thing" if adjusting seems difficult. Start slowly and build your *Shabbat* observance as you are able. The Lord will be pleased with your efforts.

Making the Challah

T.G.I.F., the acronym for "Thank God It's Friday," has become a popular expression, articulating relief that the work week is drawing to a close and the weekend is (finally!) in sight. In our home it means that pleasant aromas are on their way, beginning with the making of the Sabbath bread, the *challah*. You can buy *challah* in almost any supermarket nowadays, but if you can, we heartily recommend making it. The invention of the bread machine has made this particularly easy.

Most bread machines offer a recipe for egg bread or holiday braided bread, and using the machine bypasses much of the mess. The mixing and the first rising are done in the machine; the braiding and second rising are then done by hand. Some say that in braiding the bread you infuse it with all your hopes and prayers; certainly there is something wonderfully creative in taking a formless lump of dough and transforming it into a carefully braided work of art. That in itself is a reminder of what God is busy doing in us as he fashions us into the image of his son. After the bread has risen, we glaze the *challah* with egg white and decorate it with sesame or poppy seeds to make the finished appearance of the bread a delight to the eyes. Recipes for *challah*—both hand-made and machine-aided—can be found in Appendix A/Menus and Recipes.

When a *challah* is made under *kosher* supervision, a small piece of the dough (called the "*challah*") is taken from the loaf and burned in the oven. This comes from the command of Num. 15:20, 21: "Set aside from your first dough a cake as a gift. . . . From your first dough you will give ADONAI a portion as a gift through all your generations." During the time of the Temple, the priests (*cohanim*) were given this cake, this portion of the dough. Today this procedure is called "taking *challah*." Since there are no priests, an olive-sized portion of the dough is burned by placing it in a piece of aluminum foil at the bottom of the oven in remembrance of this commandment.

Tradition instructs us to bake two *challot* (plural for *challah*) to signify the double portion of manna that God provided every Friday in the wilderness (Exod. 16:5). Fresh from the oven, the golden loaves cool on wire racks and permeate our home with their glorious fragrance. (Frankly, the aroma alone is enough to bring work to a halt!)

The Table is Set

The white linen cloth billows and then settles calmly upon the dining room table. Wrinkles are smoothed to flawless perfection. Cloth napkins are threaded into napkin rings and the dishes are set in place. Wine goblets are carefully arranged at each setting and a tray bearing two *challot* is covered with a festive, decorative cloth.

It took the Rubins almost two decades, but a few years ago we finally decided to purchase a special set of dishes that we use only for *Shabbat* and the holy days. On other nights we use our every-day dishes; but the "fancy" ones come out Friday afternoon when the *Shabbat* table is set, to remind us that we are approaching a unique day, set apart from the rest of the week.

Like a Bridegroom Adorned for a Bride

Around the same time we got the dishes, we decided to "dress" for *Shabbat*. The traditional song *"L'khah Dodi"* (commonly translated, "Come, My Beloved") urges us to welcome the *Shabbat* as a queen. Other traditions present the Sabbath as a bride and the Jewish people as her bridegroom. For such an occasion one usually shows respect by dressing in fine array. But the thought of getting all dressed up sounded like anything but restful! Clearly some Solomonic wisdom was needed. We read of one solution to the problem of how to dress for *Shabbat*.

This solution appealed to our notion of the Sabbath as both a special day but a relaxing one, too. We bought each member of our family a *Shabbat* robe, a loose-fitting festive garment that we wear only on Friday nights. In donning these robes, we get a feeling of dressing up and also of resting. The wearing of a white *kippah* (skullcap) also accompanies the wedding-feast tradition. The *Shabbat* robe solution can work for family members of all ages. Even young children who do not like to "get dressed up" usually enjoy "dressing up," or wearing costumes. The *Shabbat* robe is the costume we wear as we imagine our home is a palace where we are about to enjoy a wedding feast!

Shabbat Dinner

And a feast it is. The *Sabbath* is not an evening to microwave a frozen dinner. It is not the occasion to order take-out. It is not the time to clean out the refrigerator of leftovers. This is a night for freshly prepared food—and lots of it. One of the most enjoyable things about Friday night is the meal itself. If we imagine that the Sabbath Queen is joining us, a feast is certainly in order! Menus for *Shabbat* dinner vary around the world.

The Rubins have adopted the weekly Friday-night-chicken tradition; another traditional *Shabbat* meal in North America is brisket, while in other places fish is favored (see Appendix A/Menus and Recipes). Elaborate preparation can add to the gleeful anticipation and thorough enjoyment of the *Shabbat* meal.

Two musts for the Sabbath meal are *challah* and wine (or grape juice). Over these two elements the blessings will be recited or sung, following the lighting of the *Shabbat* candles.

Candle-lighting

Light was the first thing God created. In saying "Let there be light" (Gen. 1:3), he set in motion this wondrous universe. So the lighting of candles, traditionally performed eighteen minutes before sundown, marks the beginning of our wondrous Sabbath celebration. Although this *mitzvah* (commandment) is not literally decreed in the *Torah*, it has become in many respects the symbol of *Shabbat*; many who observe little else in God's law derive great comfort and peace from this simple act. Although commonly understood as the realm of women only, the privilege applies equally to men. Single men or men whose wives are out of town can, and indeed *ought* to light *Shabbat* candles in the absence of a woman to do so. Most commonly, two candles are lit. Traditionally, the two represent the Sabbath commands: *observe* and *remember*, but variations abound in terms of numbers of candles. Some women light two—for their husbands and themselves—then add one for each of their children. Some Messianic Jewish believers have picked up the practice of lighting three candles. Most agree that two is the minimum. (*Shabbat* candles may be found in a Jewish gift store or market or through Messianic Jewish Resources International; see Appendix C.)

In our home we try to set out the Sabbath candles early on Friday. Standing guard like soldiers in dress whites, they are a reminder of the glow the candles will bring to our home later, as the sky darkens.

Let the Sabbath Begin!

The work week is behind us. Preparations have been made. The house is clean (well, as clean as it's going to get). Dinner is ready. The table is set. The robes are donned. The guests have arrived. Greet one another with "*Shabbat Shalom*," the Hebrew greeting for the Sabbath, and enter the Sabbath experience.

Erev Shabbat (Eve of the Sabbath)

Order of Service

It is not our desire to encumber anyone with hard and fast rules, or with the sort of rigidity that starches out blessing. It is our goal to help you to enjoy observing God's commandment to remember the Sabbath—to keep it holy. If you are new to Sabbath observance, begin with a few traditions. If Hebrew is difficult for you, don't get caught up struggling with the language. Try the English along with a few words of transliteration, like seasoning, to add flavor. We have provided the Hebrew, English transliteration, and English translation in each case. Sometimes we give only the first sentence in Hebrew and transliteration and then the full text in English.

We have also labeled as "optional" certain embellished aspects of the service which beginners might want to wait awhile before including. Remember, too, that the order of the Sabbath home observance is not inspired or infallible; pick and choose, arrange and rearrange and discover what works best for your family.

Hadlakat Haneyrot (Lighting the Candles)

As we have already discussed, candles are traditionally lit about 18 minutes before sundown; this is to be certain that a cushion of time prevents us from accidentally lighting the candles *after* the Sabbath has begun. Most Jewish calendars include candle-lighting times for many prominent cities. More specific information can be downloaded from the Internet if your city is not included in the calendars.

The women of the house gather together to light the candles. Married women usually cover their heads; unmarried women do not. Strike a match and light each candle. Cover your eyes as you pray; then open your eyes and enjoy the warm candle light.

בָּרוּךְ אַתָּה יְיָ, אֱלֹהֵינוּ מֶלֶךְ הָעוֹלָם, אֲשֶׁר
קִדְּשָׁנוּ בְּמִצְוֹתָיו וְצִוָּנוּ לְהַדְלִיק נֵר שֶׁל שַׁבָּת.

Barukh atah Adonai, Eloheynu melekh ha'olam, asher kidshanu b'mitzvotav v'tzivanu l'hadlik neyr shel Shabbat.

Blessed are you, Lord our God, King of the universe, who has set us apart by his commandments and commanded us to kindle the Sabbath lights.

(As we already mentioned, the Bible does not specifically command the lighting of the candles, but this tradition is considered a fulfillment of the command to set the Sabbath day apart.)

Optional Prayers
Other traditional prayers may also be spoken following the blessing over the candles.

יְהִי רָצוֹן מִלְפָנֶיךָ. יְיָ אֱלֹהֵנוּ וֵאלֹהֵי אֲבוֹתֵינוּ.
שֶׁיִבָּנֶה בֵית הַמִקְדָשׁ בִּמְהֵרָה בְיָמֵינוּ.
וְתֵן חֶלְקֵנוּ בְתוֹרָתֶךָ. וְשָׁם נַעֲבָדְךָ בְּיִרְאָה
כִּימֵי עוֹלָם וּכְשָׁנִים קַדְמוֹנִיוֹת.
וְעָרְבָה לַיְיָ מִנְחַת יְהוּדָה וִירוּשָׁלַיִם
כִּימֵי עוֹלָם וּכְשָׁנִים קַדְמוֹנִיוֹת.

Y'hi ratzon milfaneykha, ADONAI Eloheynu vey'lohey avoteynu, sheyibaneh beyt HaMikdash bimheyrah v'yameynu, v'teyn chelkeynu b'Toratekha. V'sham na'avadkha b'yir'ah kimey olam ukhshanim kadmoniyot. V'arvah l'ADONAI minchat Y'hudah viyrushalayim kimey olam ukh'shanim kadmoniyot.

May it be your will, LORD our God and God of our fathers, that the Temple will be rebuilt soon in our time, and grant our involvement with your *Torah*. And there we will serve you reverently as in days gone by, in olden times. And may the service of Judah and Jerusalem be pleasing to you. There we will serve you reverently as in days gone by, in olden times.

יְהִי רָצוֹן מִלְפָנֶךָ. יְיָ אֱלֹהֵי וֵאלֹהֵי אֲבוֹתַי.
שֶׁתְחוֹנֵן אוֹתִי [וְאֶת-אִישִׁי וְאֶת-בָּנַי] וְאֶת-כָּל-קְרוֹבַי
וְתַשְׁלִים בָּתֵּינוּ וְתַשְׁכֵּן שְׁכִינָתְךָ בֵּינֵינוּ.
וְזַכֵּנִי לְגַדֵּל בָּנִים וּבְנֵי בָנִים חֲכָמִים וּמְאִירִים
אֶת-הָעוֹלָם בַּתוֹרָה וּבְמַעֲשִׂים טוֹבִים וְהָאֵר
נֵרֵנוּ שֶׁלֹא יִכְבֶּה לְעוֹלָם וָעֶד. וְהָאֵר פָּנֶיךָ וְנִוָּשֵׁעָה. אָמֵן.

*Y'hi ratzon milfaneykha, ADONAI Elohai vey'lohey avotai, shetchoneyn oti
(ve'et-ishi, ve'et-banai) ve'et-kol-k'rovai, v'tashlim bateynu v'tashkeyn
sh'khinatkha beyneynu. V'zakeyni l'gaddeyl banim uvney vanim chakhamim
um'irim et-ha'olam baTorah uv'ma'asim tovim v'ha'eyr neyreynu shelo
yikhbeh l'olam va'ed. V'ha'eyr paneykha v'nivvashey'ah. Ameyn.*

May it be your will, LORD my God and God of my fathers, to be gracious to me
(and to my husband and children) and to all my family, crowning our home
with the feeling of your divine presence dwelling among us. Make me worthy
to raise learned children and grandchildren who will dazzle with world with
Torah and goodness, and ensure that the glow of our lives will never be
dimmed. Show us the glow of your face and we will be saved. Amen.

Shalom Aleykhem (We Bring Peace to You)

One lovely tradition holds that two angels accompany a Jewish man home to witness his
celebration of *Shabbat*. From this tradition, a beautiful song of welcome begins many *erev
Shabbat* observances. Below we have included one verse (see Appendix B for the music).

שָׁלוֹם עֲלֵיכֶם מַלְאֲכֵי הַשָּׁרֵת, מַלְאֲכֵי עֶלְיוֹן
מִמֶּלֶךְ מַלְכֵי הַמְּלָכִים, הַקָּדוֹשׁ בָּרוּךְ הוּא.

*Shalom aleykhem mal'akhey hashareyt mal'akhey elyon
mimelekh malkhey hamlakhim hakkadosh barukh hu.*

Peace unto you, ministering angels, messengers of the Most High,
of the supreme King of kings, the Holy One, blessed be he.

Here are the rest of the verses in English:
Come in peace, messengers of peace, messengers of the Most High,
of the supreme King of kings, the Holy One, blessed be he.
Bless me with peace, messengers of peace, messengers of the Most High,
of the supreme King of kings, the Holy One, blessed be he.
And may your departure be in peace, messengers of peace, messengers of the
Most High, of the supreme King of kings, the Holy One, blessed be he.

A Woman of Valor: Eyshet Chayil (Prov. 31:10–31)

The heart of the home is the woman; tradition considers her the stabilizing force of Jewish family life. When we added the recitation of this Proverb to our *Shabbat* observance, a certain wife experienced it as a burden . . . until a certain husband told her that she indeed fulfilled this portrait better than anyone he knew. Use this as a time to bless the woman of the house . . . as well as a time to teach the children the value of a godly wife.

> Who can find a capable wife?
> > Her value is far beyond that of pearls.
> Her husband trusts her from his heart,
> > and she will prove a great asset to him.
> She works to bring him good, not harm,
> > all the days of her life.
>
> She procures a supply of wool and flax
> > and works with willing hands.
> She is like those merchant vessels,
> > bringing her food from far away.
> It's still dark when she rises to give food to her household
> > and orders to the young women serving her.
>
> She considers a field, then buys it,
> > and from her earnings she plants a vineyard.
> She gathers her strength around her
> > and throws herself into her work.
> She sees that her business affairs go well;
> > her lamp stays lit at night.
>
> She puts her hands to the staff with the flax;
> > her fingers hold the spinning rod.
> She reaches out to embrace the poor
> > and opens her arms to the needy.
> When it snows, she has no fear for her household;
> > since all of them are doubly clothed.

She makes her own quilts;
> she is clothed in fine linen and purple.

Her husband is known at the city gates
> when he sits with the leaders of the land.

She makes linen garments and sells them;
> she supplies the merchants with sashes.

Clothed with strength and dignity,
> she can laugh at the days to come.

When she opens her mouth, she speaks wisely;
> on her tongue is loving instruction.

She watches how things go in her house,
> not eating the bread of idleness.

Her children arise; they make her happy;
> her husband too, as he praises her:

"Many women have done wonderful things,
> but you surpass them all!"

Charm can lie, beauty can vanish,
> but a woman who fears *Adonai* should be praised.

Give her a share in what she produces;
> let her works speak her praises at the city gates.

Birkhat HaBanim (Blessing the Children)

Prevailing opinions in psychology have finally recognized something that Sabbath observers have known for generations: blessing your children is key to both their mental and spiritual health. Part of the Friday evening tradition, following the blessing of the wife through the reading of Proverbs 31, is *Birkhat HaBanim*: Blessing the Children.

There are three blessings: one specifically for sons, one for daughters and the traditional Aaronic benediction (see Num. 6:4), which is spoken over all the children. We have two daughters, and we have always said the blessing with our hands upon their heads.

Blessing for the boys

יְשִׂמְךָ אֱלֹהִים כְּאֶפְרַיִם וְכִמְנַשֶּׁה.

Y'simkha Elohim k'Efrayim v'khimnasheh

May God make you like Ephraim and Manasseh.

Blessing for the girls

יְשִׂמֵךְ אֱלֹהִים כְּשָׂרָה, רִבְקָה, רָחֵל, וְלֵאָה.

Y'simeykh Elohim k'Sarah, Rivkah, Racheyl v'Ley'ah

May God make you like Sarah, Rebecca, Rachel and Leah

The Aaronic Benediction (for all children)

יְבָרֶכְךָ יְיָ וְיִשְׁמְרֶךָ.
יָאֵר יְיָ פָּנָיו אֵלֶיךָ וִיחֻנֶּךָּ.
יִשָּׂא יְיָ פָּנָיו אֵלֶיךָ.
וְיָשֵׂם לְךָ שָׁלוֹם.

Y'varekh'kha Adonai v'yishm'rekha
Ya'eyr Adonai panav eyleykha vichunekha
Yisa Adonai panav eyleykha
V'yaseym l'kha shalom.

May Adonai bless you and keep you.
May Adonai make his face shine on you and show you his favor.
May Adonai lift up his face toward you and give you peace. (Num. 6:24–26)

Next comes a Rubin-specific tradition that you won't find in an Orthodox, Conservative or Reform (or even Messianic!) Sabbath service: blessing of the children by giving them their allowance. Let us explain. A few years back, in our daughters' early teen years, they became a little impatient having Dad place his hands on their heads and bless them. They were getting taller; it felt childish and even a little embarrassing—

especially when there were guests. In order to associate this process with instant and undeniable blessing, we decided to append the giving of allowance to this part of the service. As you can imagine the girls always look forward to this particular blessing!

Kiddush (Blessing Over the Wine)

The *kiddush* (a word meaning "sanctification" or "holiness") is a prayer recited over a cup of wine (or grape juice). It is usually recited by a man, although the entire family may participate. Even when the kids were small, we included them in the blessing by having "kids' wine"—sparkling juice or flavored soda. The first part of the prayer is non-specific for the Sabbath, the generic blessing over wine. The second part, which we have listed as optional, is specifically for *Shabbat*.

One interesting custom concerning the *kiddush* is for the *challah* to be covered during the recitation. Why? Tradition explains that it is so the *challah* is not insulted that we say the *kiddush* over the wine *before* we say the blessing over the *challah*. The underlying message is that peace and harmony should always accompany the Sabbath celebration.

Recite or sing while holding up the goblets of wine

בָּרוּךְ אַתָּה יְיָ, אֱלֹהֵינוּ מֶלֶךְ הָעוֹלָם. בּוֹרֵא פְּרִי הַגָּפֶן.

Barukh atah Adonai, Eloheynu melekh ha'olam, borey p'ri hagafen.

Blessed are you, Lord our God, king of the universe, creator of the fruit of the vine.

Optional Readings

Now the vineyard of *Adonai -Tzva'ot* is the house of Isra'el,
and the men of Y'hudah are the plant he delighted in (Isa. 5:7a).

I am the vine and you are the branches. Those who stay united with me, and I with them, are the ones who bear much fruit; because apart from me you can't do a thing. This is how my father is glorified—in your bearing much fruit; this is how you will prove to be my *talmidim* (John 15:5, 8).

Hand-Washing

N'tilat Yadayim is a common practice within Judaism. During the time of Yeshua, the practices and rules had begun to mount up so that they became burdensome. Indeed, Yeshua scolded some religious leaders for being inordinately judgmental on this subject, as illustrated by their criticism of Yeshua's *talmidim* (disciples) in Matt. 15:2. Still, Yeshua engaged in this practice himself, even extending it to the washing of his disciples' feet at his last *Pesach seder* (Passover meal).

N'tilat Yadayim is a ceremonial cleansing, not really a complete washing. You'll need a cup and a bowl and perhaps an extra napkin or small towel. Pour some water over your hands from a cup into a small bowl. Pass the cup and bowl around to each person.

Recite (before drying hands)

בָּרוּךְ אַתָּה יְיָ, אֱלֹהֵינוּ מֶלֶךְ הָעוֹלָם.
אֲשֶׁר קִדְּשָׁנוּ בְּמִצְוֹתָיו וְצִוָּנוּ עַל נְטִלַת יָדָים.

Barukh atah ADONAI, Eloheynu melekh ha'olam, asher kidshanu b'mitzvotav v'tzivanu al n'tilat yadayim.

Blessed are you, LORD our God, king of the universe, who set us apart by his commandments and commanded us regarding the washing of hands.

Optional Rreading

> Who may go up to the mountain of *ADONAI*?
> Who can stand in his holy place?
> Those with clean hands and pure hearts,
> who don't make vanities the purpose of their lives
> or swear oaths just to deceive.
> They will receive a blessing from *ADONAI*
> and justice from God, who saves them (Ps. 24:3–5).

Hamotzi (Blessing the Bread)

Tradition has it that there should be no talking from the prayer before the hand-washing until the blessing over the loaves of *challah* has been made.

The father lifts the two *challot* and recites or chants:

בָּרוּךְ אַתָּה יְיָ, אֱלֹהֵינוּ מֶלֶךְ הָעוֹלָם.
הַמוֹצִי לֶחֶם מִן הָאָרֶץ.

Barukh atah ADONAI, *Eloheynu melekh ha'olam, hamotzi lechem min ha'aretz.*

Blessed are you, LORD our God, king of the universe, who brings forth bread from the earth.

The bread may be cut or torn (we are tearers) into small pieces. The pieces are salted to remind us of the salting of the sacrifices (Lev. 2:13) and also because salt was part of the ratifying of any covenant. The pieces of bread are distributed and eaten by family and guests. The words of Yeshua, "I am the bread which has come down from heaven" (John 6:41), and his admonition to his *talmidim*, "You are salt for the Land" (Matt. 5:13), come to mind as we savor the taste.

The Shabbat Meal

Relax, relish and recline. Do not gobble, scarf or bolt. The relaxed atmosphere of *Shabbat* is your reward after a bustling week of work, study, and activity.

Let your conversation be of God, family, friends and Scripture—perhaps the *Torah* portion or related Scripture passages. If you have guests, use the conversation during the meal to draw them into the bosom of your family. Food is one of God's most generous gifts to humankind and we are blessed, too, to be able to share it with friends and strangers. In our home we have a saying: On *Shabbat* there are no calories!

Being Jewish, we have been brought up with the assurance that the unforgivable sin is not having enough food. On *Shabbat* the order of the day is *plenty*! This accomplishes two things. It provides an atmosphere of generosity toward those at the table and it affords ample leftovers so that the woman of the house does not have to disturb her *Shabbat* rest with further preparation of food until the Sabbath is over.

So linger over this feast—there's nothing to hurry off to! Again, we remind you to look in Appendix A for menu suggestions and recipes.

Birkat HaMazon (Grace After the Meal)

It is customary to follow the meal with the singing of *z'mirot*, special Sabbath songs or hymns. Some congregations have *erev Shabbat* services, and of course we would encourage you to attend and enjoy the fellowship. But if you remain at home, perhaps a family Bible study would be an appropriate activity to follow the meal; this can be geared toward the children. You may want to read a passage and then invite interpretation. Or you may conduct a question-and-answer session directed to the children's levels.

The Grace After the Meal is a traditional prayer that follows the eating of a meal. It can be quite lengthy when recited in its entirety. Below we have included only a few lines of *Birkat HaMazon* (see Bibliography for prayer books that contain the full blessings).

בָּרוּךְ אַתָּה יְיָ, אֱלֹהֵינוּ מֶלֶךְ הָעוֹלָם.
הַזָּן אֶת הָעוֹלָם כֻּלוֹ, בְּטוּבוֹ.
בְּחֵן בְּחֶסֶד וּבְרַחֲמִים.
הוּא נֹתֵן לֶחֶם לְכָל בָּשָׂר, כִּי לְעוֹלָם חַסְדוֹ.

הָרַחֲמָן הוּא יַנְחִילֵנוּ יוֹם שֶׁכֻּלוֹ שַׁבָּת
וּמְנוּחָה לְחַיֵּי הָעוֹלָמִים.

Barukh atah ADONAI, *Eloheynu melekh ha'olam, hazzan et ha'olam kullo, b'tuvo, b'cheyn, b'chesed uv'rachamim. Hu noteyn lechem l'khol basar, ki l'olam chasddo.*

Harachaman hu yanchileynu yom shekulo Shabbat um'nuchah l'chayey ha'olamim.

Blessed are you, LORD our God, king of the universe, who feeds the entire world in his goodness—with love, kindness, and mercy. He gives food to all people, because his kindness lasts forever.

May the Merciful God let us inherit the *Shabbat* of the World to Come, which will be a complete rest day forever.

The Day of Shabbat

God's commandment concerning *Shabbat* is found in Lev. 23:3:

> Work is to be done on six days; but the seventh day is a *Shabbat* of complete rest, a holy convocation; you are not to do any kind of work; it is a *Shabbat* for ADONAI, even in your homes.

We have discussed and have begun to enter into the Sabbath rest. Now about that holy convocation.

God created his people for fellowship; we are meant to get together to worship him. Saturday morning services give us an opportunity to draw together, be lifted up and, most important, to glorify God. In coming together for worship, we are not only stepping away from the world and its distractions and concerns, but we are stepping into a world-apart—an oasis of rest, a place to express our love for and devotion to God. This is where we lift our voices as one and proclaim that God is one and his name is one.

The synagogue service is not a spectator sport; we encourage everyone to learn how to participate in the service. A complete knowledge of Hebrew is a high and lofty goal and some may be farther along than others, but even if Hebrew is "all Greek to you," hearing and following along with the transliteration will help you learn how to recite many of the ancient blessings. Know that, as you learn, you are a link in a long chain of God's people who have spoken these same words, have sought God as you seek him, and have been blessed through his gift of the Sabbath.

The Synagogue Service

Describing the synagogue service is a book in itself. For our purposes, we will just touch on some of the salient points for those who are not familiar with them.

Tallit/Kippah (Prayer shawl/headcovering)

Depending on the congregation, these are provided for men to wear. You may wish to purchase your own *tallit* and *kippah* if you regularly attend a service where these are worn. (See copyright for MJRI address and order line.)

Siddur (Prayer book)

Traditional synagogues use prayer books, from which ancient prayers are read or chanted. Many Messianic congregations use either traditional or Messianic *siddurs* for the liturgical aspects of their services. (See Bibliography.)

Sh'ma (Deut. 6:4)

Even the least liturgical synagogue includes the chanting of this, the universal confession of Judaism: "Hear, Isra'el, ADONAI our God, ADONAI is one" (Deut. 6:4). When Messiah Yeshua was asked, "Which is the most important *mitzvah* [commandment] of them all?," he answered, "The most important is, *'Sh'ma Yisra'el, ADONAI Eloheinu, ADONAI echad* [Hear O Isra'el, the LORD our God, the LORD is one]'" (Mark 12:29).

Amidah or *Sh'moneh Esreyh* ("Standing Prayer," also known as the "Eighteen Benedictions")

These prayers are affirmations concerning God, expressing confidence in him as the God who raises the dead and grants eternal life. These are recited or silently meditated upon while standing.

Kaddish (Meaning "sanctified", a prayer magnifying God)

Sometimes mistakenly thought of as a prayer for the dead, since it is recited by mourners, the *Kaddish* actually is a prayer which glorifies God as Creator, calling upon him to establish his kingdom on earth and to bring peace.

Torah Service

We stand when the Ark (Closet containing the *Torah* scrolls) in the front of the synagogue is opened and the *Torah* is removed from it. Before the readings, the *Torah* is paraded around the synagogue. At this time reverence is shown for God's Word by touching the cover of the *Torah* with the *tzitzit* (fringe) of the *tallit* or with the *siddur* and bringing it back to one's lips. Then the weekly portion is read. The service includes the following main parts:

Aliyah (calling someone up to read prayers before the *Torah* reading)
Torah Readings/Blessings before and after
Haftarah Readings/Blessings before and after
B'rit Chadashah Readings/Blessings before and after
(The *B'rit Chadashah* blessings and readings only appear in a Messianic synagogue service)

Other prayers are spoken or chanted during the *Torah* service, praising God for his Word and recalling the miraculous events surround the giving of the *Torah* through the hand of Moses.

Aleynu (Meaning, "It is our duty")
>This is a prayer recognizing the distinct calling of Israel and expressing the confidence that one day God will reign over the earth.

Aaronic Benediction (Num. 6:24–26; This is the same as the prayer we recite at home on *erev Shabbat*; see page 22)

Kiddush and Oneg Shabbat (Food, again!)

We are convinced that our congregation does one thing better than any other—eat! Sharing a meal as a congregation is not always possible, but it is certainly worth the effort to pull it off. One of our members has divided the congregation into four food teams, corresponding to the first four Saturdays in the month. (Fifth Saturdays occur four times a year; we do a pot-luck on those days.)

On the designated week, the food team captain coordinates the bringing of the various parts of the meal: appetizers and salads, main dishes, side dishes, and desserts and drinks. (Assignments vary so the same people are not always responsible to bring the main dish, etc.) It may seem like a burden to bring food to services, but remember, it's only once a month. The rest of the month you are the guest of your fellow congregants!

The best thing about the congregational meals (besides "Bubbe" [Grandma] Belle's brisket!) is the fellowship we share. Because we follow our formal service with a short discussion of the message and/or readings, we move along to the social hall, our minds stimulated by the challenging exchange of ideas. Often such conversation continues over the delicious meal. Instead of folks departing quickly and heading their separate ways, many linger long into the afternoon.

If your congregation is the rushing-out sort, why not at least offer bagels and coffee to encourage the fellowship to continue!

The REST of the Day

Remember, in biblical reckoning a day goes from sundown to sundown. If you are a typical modern-day over-achiever you will probably need to *remember to rest* as Saturday wears on. Here are some suggestions.

Activities for the REST of the Day

- Napping (there's nothing more restful than sleep!)
- Bible study (Certainly anything is appropriate, but the book of Proverbs makes for lively discussion for family members of all ages.)
- Praying
- Visiting (This can be a neighborly visit or even a visit to a shut-in unable to fellowship otherwise; visiting the sick is a *mitzvah* (commandment) any day of the week, but especially on *Shabbat.*)
- Walking (This can take the form of a leisurely neighborhood stroll or a hike in the country.)
- Reading (preferably something restful and edifying)
- Spending time with your family (With all the statistics about how little time parents and children spend together, here is your chance to really catch up!)
- Listening to music or making your own
- Celebrating anything that is a gift from God

What to Eat (yes, eat) the Rest of the Day

In case some of you are wondering, "Do these people think of ANYTHING besides food?!," let us reiterate that food is a gift from God and an important aspect of any celebration. (Have you ever considered that when God declared a celebration it was always called a "feast"?) But here are just two suggestions concerning the Saturday evening dinner.

An old culinary tradition among observant Jews is to prepare a slow-cooking dish called *Cholent*, which will be ready for Saturday eating without having to go to a lot of trouble during this restful day. *Cholent* is a hearty stew that gets tastier as the day goes on. (Recipe is included in Appendix A.)

Another solution, more suited to warm weather, is to make a light dinner on Saturday night—something that requires little to no preparation. Foods might include salads of all kinds, fruit, tuna or turkey sandwiches, hard-boiled eggs, sour cream, cheeses or whatever your family's favorite thrown-together meal consists of. Remember the guiding rule here is not to make a great labor out of dinner preparation on the Sabbath day.

Havdalah (Separation)

They say that all good things must come to an end, and so it is with the *Shabbat*—at least for this week. But to make the transition from *Shabbat* into the week a little easier, there is a friendly little ceremony called *Havdalah*. *Havdalah* comes from the Hebrew word *l'havdil*, "to separate," and recognizes that God has made a separation between the sacred and the secular, between light and darkness, and between *Shabbat* and the rest of the days of the week. In performing *Havdalah* we recognize that we are making a transition and bidding a fond farewell to God's Sabbath. Traditionally, the *Havdalah* ceremony takes place after sunset, when work may begin again.

In order to do *Havdalah*, several items are needed:

a *Havdalah* candle (a special braided candle having a minimum of two wicks—
   Havdalah candles can be found in the resources section of Appendix C)
   or two candles that are put together

a wine cup and saucer

wine or grape juice

spices (sweet spices like cloves)—These are sometimes housed in a decorative
   ceremonial spice box.

The Wine

Begin by filling the wine glass full to overflowing. One tradition holds that this reminds us of the psalmist's expression, "You anoint my head with oil from an overflowing cup" (Ps. 23:5b). The overflowed wine will soon come into play. The *Havdalah* prayer is made up of several parts. Usually the ceremony is begun with the reading or singing of Isa. 12:2, 3. The well-known Messianic song "Behold, God is My Salvation" by Stuart Dauermann, based on this verse, is a lively way to begin (see Appendix B).

There are several other songs that include the verse about joyously drawing water from the springs of salvation that also work well. Another Scripture passage that is often quoted as part of the *Havdalah* ceremony is the conclusion of the Purim narrative from Esther 8:16, "For the Jews, all was light, gladness, joy and honor" to which we add, "So may it be for us as well."

Next comes the blessing over the wine, the same one that we recited over the goblet on the previous evening:

בָּרוּךְ אַתָּה יְיָ, אֱלֹהֵינוּ מֶלֶךְ הָעוֹלָם. בּוֹרֵא פְּרִי הַגָּפֶן.

Barukh atah ADONAI, *Eloheynu melekh ha'olam, borey p'ri hagafen.*

Blessed are you, LORD our God, king of the universe, creator of the fruit
of the vine.

Pass the wine goblet around, letting everyone take a sip; this is the first way we
fondly remember the Sabbath.

The Spices

Just as the spices leave a fragrant aroma in our minds, so does the Sabbath leave an
essence of sweetness as it leaves us.

Take the spices in your right hand and recite the following blessing

בָּרוּךְ אַתָּה יְיָ, אֱלֹהֵינוּ מֶלֶךְ הָעוֹלָם.
בּוֹרֵא מִינֵי בְשָׂמִים.

Barukh atah ADONAI, *Eloheynu melekh ha'olam, borey miney v'samim.*

Blessed are you, LORD our God, king of the universe, creator of the fruit of
various kinds of spices.

Pass the spices around, letting everyone sniff their sweetness; this is the second way we
fondly remember the Sabbath.

The Fire

Light the multi-wick *Havdalah* candle and hold it over the saucer and pray

בָּרוּךְ אַתָּה יְיָ, אֱלֹהֵינוּ מֶלֶךְ הָעוֹלָם.
בּוֹרֵא מְאוֹרֵי הָאֵשׁ.

Barukh atah ADONAI, *Eloheynu melekh ha'olam, borey m'orey ha'eysh.*

Blessed are you, LORD our God, king of the universe, creator of the lights of fire.

As the candle burns and the blessing is recited, it is customary to bring one's hands near to the flame, making a very loose fist, nails facing up. As the light of the candle shines on the fingernails, a shadow is cast into the palm, displaying the difference between light and shadow and preparing us for the final *Havdalah* prayer.

Concluding Blessing
Recite (while still holding the candle)

בָּרוּךְ אַתָּה יְיָ, אֱלֹהֵינוּ מֶלֶךְ הָעוֹלָם,
הַמַּבְדִּיל בֵּין קֹדֶשׁ לְחֹל,
בֵּין אוֹר לְחֹשֶׁךְ. בֵּין יִשְׂרָאֵל לָעַמִּים.
בֵּין יוֹם הַשְּׁבִיעִי לְשֵׁשֶׁת יְמֵי הַמַּעֲשֶׂה.
בָּרוּךְ אַתָּה יְיָ, הַמַּבְדִּיל בֵּין קֹדֶשׁ לְחֹל.

Barukh atah ADONAI, Eloheynu melekh ha'olam, hamavdil beyn kodesh l'chol, beyn or l'choshekh, beyn Yisra'el la'amim, beyn yom hashviy'i l'sheyshet y'mey hama'aseh. Barukh atah ADONAI, hamavdil beyn kodesh l'chol.

Blessed are you, LORD our God, king of the universe, who makes a distinction between the sacred and the secular, between light and darkness, between Israel and the other nations, between the seventh day and the six working days. Blessed are you, LORD, who makes a distinction between the sacred and the secular.

Now extinguish the candle in the wine which overflowed into the saucer.

HaMavdil (The Separation)
Recite (We have included only the English)

He who makes a distinction between the sacred and the secular, may he also pardon our sins. May he proliferate our children and our wealth like the sand, and like the stars at night.

Twilight has arrived like the shade of a palm tree; I call to God who gives me everything. The watchman says morning comes, but night, too.

Your righteousness is as great as Mount Tabor; please ignore, disregard my sins. May they be as yesterday—gone—like a watch in the night.

The time when I would bring offerings is long gone. If only I had rest! I am so tired of sighing, I weep every night.

Do not allow my voice to be stifled; open the gate on high for me; for my head is soaked with dew, my locks with the drops of the night.

Grant my prayer, revered and awesome one; I implore you, bring redemption, at dusk, in the evening, in the dark of night.

I am calling you, God, save me; show me life's scheme. Keep me from poverty, by day and by night.

Purify the defilement of my actions, lest those who incite me ask where is the God who made me, who can inspire hymns in the night.

We are as clay in your hand; please forgive out petty and our major sins. Each day tells a story, and each night.

Prayer Requests

This is a good time to pray for specific issues in the upcoming week. Ask each family member or friend to pray for something that can be reported on at the close of the following Sabbath. You might even want to keep a r/unning prayer journal for *Havdalah*.

A Final Song

It is traditional to sing the Passover song *Eliyahu HaNavi* (Elijah the Prophet; see Appendix B) at the end of *Havdalah*, since it is thought that Elijah would not come back during *Shabbat*. Now we are free to watch for his return.

One Final Wish

Just as we greeted one another with *Shabbat Shalom* at the beginning of the Sabbath, we finish the *Havdalah* ceremony by wishing one another *Shavu'ah Tov*! (A good week!)

A Few More Words

It has been our goal in this short book to encourage you as you begin your own *Shabbat* celebration or as you continue to learn about this blessing of God. Remember the words of Moshe (Moses) as he addressed the children of Israel.

> For this *mitzvah* which I am giving you today is not too hard for you, nor is it beyond your reach. It isn't in the sky, so that you need to ask, 'Who will go up into the sky for us, bring it to us and make us hear it so that we can obey it?' Likewise, it isn't beyond the sea, so that you need to ask, 'Who will cross the sea for us, bring it to us and make us hear it, so that we can obey it?' On the contrary, the word is very close to you—in your mouth, even in your heart; therefore you can do it!" (Deut. 30:11–14)

We have tried to bring near to you the blessing of celebrating the *Shabbat*. You *can* do it!

Appendix A
Menu and Recipes for Shabbat

Menu Suggestions

These are suggestions by category. There is no inspired menu for *Shabbat*; you are welcome to try any of these. Dishes with asterisks are included in the Recipes section.

Starter suggestions
Challah*

Gefilte Fish (Available in the supermarket. Yes, you can make it yourself, but I have never done it, nor do I intend to: life is too short.)

Chicken Soup

Green Salad

Cold Soup (especially for summer evenings; e.g., beet borscht, available in the supermarket)

Main Dish suggestions
Roast Chicken (No recipe needed here, just don't forget the garlic)

Beef Brisket*

Broiled Fish

Side Dish suggestions
Potatoes

Rice

Barley

Tabouleh (cold semolina available in easy-to-follow packages at the supermarket)

*Carrot Tzimmes**

Noodle *Kugel**

Dessert Suggestions
> Rugelach*
> Mandelbread*

(These desserts are family recipes and I look for any opportunity to share them. But, really, any dessert will do!)

Recipes

Challah (by hand)
> 1 package dry yeast
> 2 tsp sugar
> 1-1/4 cup water (lukewarm)
> 4-1/2 cups white flour (you can sift yours; I never do)
> 2 tsp salt
> 2 eggs, separated
> 2 tbsp oil or butter or margarine (melted)
> poppy seeds or sesame seeds (your choice!)

Combine yeast, sugar and 1/4 cup water and let stand for five minutes at room temperature.

Combine flour and salt in a large bowl and drop egg yolks, oil (or melted butter or margarine), yeast mixture and remaining water into a well in the middle of the dry ingredients. Mix together; then knead the mixture on a floured surface until it can be made into a ball. Place in a bowl and cover with a towel. Set it in a warm place and let it rise for an hour or until about double. Then punch down and cover again, letting it rise until double.

Punch down once again and, kneading, divide the dough into three equal parts. With floured hands, roll each part into a long snake, about 14" long. Pinch the three strands together at one end and braid. Pinch the other end together and place on a greased baking sheet. Brush the braided challah dough with the egg white and allow to rise for 1 hour.

Brush again, gently. Sprinkle sesame seeds or poppy seeds onto the *challah* and bake at 375° for 45 minutes or until browned. This makes one large loaf or two smaller loaves. (Reduce baking time for smaller loaves.)

Challah (bread machine recipe)

2 tsp yeast
2 tbsp margarine or butter
3 cups flour
2 tbsp sugar
2 tbsp non-fat dry milk
1 tsp salt
2 eggs, separated
1-1/4 cup minus 1 tbsp water (lukewarm)
All ingredients should be at room temperature

Place all the ingredients into the bread machine (except the egg whites—save them) and place the machine on the "dough" setting. After 1-1/2 hours (approximately—it will beep when done), remove the dough onto a floured surface.

With floured hands, divide the dough into three parts. Roll each part into a long snake, about 14" long. Pinch the three strands together at one end and braid. Pinch the other end together and place on a greased baking sheet. Brush the braided challah dough with the egg white and allow to rise for 1 hour.

Brush again, gently. Sprinkle sesame seeds or poppy seeds onto the challah and bake at 375° for 25 minutes or until browned. This makes a larger challah, which presents very nicely. You can also make two smallish *challot* from this recipe.

A word about raisins:

Traditionally, raisins are not present in your weekly challah and appear only in the special *challah* for *Rosh HaShanah*. However, the Rubins have become weekly raisin-*challah* people (we just add more raisins for *Rosh HaShanah*!) This is a matter of taste, but we have become very fond of our raisins and would miss them if they were absent on Friday night. (Try, too, currants or sunflower seeds—a little unorthodox, but very tasty!)

Chicken Soup

Start with a 4–5 pound chicken, or use the backs and the insides of the chickens you might be serving.

3 quarts of water	2 onions
3 carrots	2 pieces of celery, stalks and tops

| 1 tbsp salt | garlic powder: several shakes |
| 1/8 tsp pepper | 1/2 tsp dill weed |

Clean the chicken thoroughly; clean and cut up the vegetables. Add all of the ingredients to the water and bring to a boil. Then lower the heat. Simmer for 2 hours. Pour the soup through a colander, and refrigerate broth for 2–3 hours, until the fat forms a layer at the top. Save the carrots and put them aside. Remove the layer of fat and return the broth and carrots to the pot to reheat.

This will boil down to about 2 or 2-1/2 quarts of soup. If you want to stretch it a little, add more water and a few chicken bouillon cubes (when no one is looking).

Matzah Balls

1 cup *matzah* meal (from the Jewish food section in grocery)
1/2 cup water
1/3 cup vegetable oil (this is the healthiest version I know of!)
4 eggs (well, maybe not *that* healthy)
1 tsp salt
dash of pepper

Traditionally, *matzah* balls are made with "schmaltz," rendered chicken fat. But I could not in good conscience recommend such an artery-clogger in this day and age. Better to use some nice polyunsaturated oil. I promise, the *matzah* balls will still be light and fluffy. Trust me.

Brisket

This particular recipe recommends overnight marinating and four hours of roasting. You may substitute some other roasted beef if you wish.

4-1/2–5 lb. piece of brisket
2 onions (sometimes, for ease, I use dry packaged onion soup)
2 carrots (nice thin slices)

Marinade:

1/3 cup lemon juice
1 tsp salt

1/3 cup oil
1 tsp sugar or honey
1/4 cup tarragon (or other flavor) vinegar
several hefty shakes of garlic powder, or 6 sliced garlic cloves

Make the marinade first; then peel and slice the vegetables. Set the brisket and vegetables in a shallow roasting pan and pour on the marinade, coating the meat all over, as though you were rinsing off a baby. Cover the pan with aluminum foil and refrigerate overnight. When you think of it the following day, turn the meat over.

Five hours before dinner time, set the pan, still covered tightly, in a 350° oven. Roast for 4 to 4-1/2 hours, until fork-tender. Let the meat sit out for awhile after cooking to cool, which will make it easier to cut. Cut the brisket across the grain and pour the reheated marinade and vegetables over the meat before serving. Serves 10–12.

Carrot Tzimmes

Tzimmes is a word that means, well, a big to-do, as in, "It's only a little scratch on the fender; don't make such a big *tzimmes* out of it."

A carrot *tzimmes* is a sweet concoction served alongside the main dish.

1-1/2 lb. carrots	6 tbsp brown sugar
3 tbsp margarine	1/2 tsp cinnamon
1/2 tsp salt	1/4 tsp cloves
1 cup water	1 tbsp lemon juice
1/2 cup raisins	grated peel of one orange
1 cup prunes (pitted)	2 tbsp honey

Noodle Kugel

2 eggs, beaten
3 tbsp sugar
1/4 tsp cinnamon
pinch of salt
1/2 pound broad noodles, cooked and drained
4 tbsp melted butter or margarine
1/2 cup golden raisins

optional: slivered almonds
optional: 1/4 tsp nutmeg

Combine eggs, sugar, cinnamon, and salt (and nutmeg, if desired). Add them to the noodles. Add melted butter or margarine and raisins (and almonds, if desired). Mix together. Generously grease a 1-1/2 quart casserole dish and bake at 400° for 45 minutes, or until the top is lightly browned. Serves 6.

I always double this recipe and make two; freeze one and trot it out for another *Shabbat* (or anytime).

Rugelach (à la Sylvia)

When my mom, Sylvia, comes to visit, a supply of *rugelach* is her ticket into our house. Without *rugelach* we would have to send her back to Florida!

Dough
> 1 cup sweet margarine (2 sticks)
> 2 cups unsifted all-purpose flour
> 1 egg yolk
> 3/4 cup sour cream

Filling
> 3/4 cup golden raisins
> 1/2 cup sugar
> 2 tsp cinnamon
> 1/2 cup chopped walnuts

Glaze
> 1 egg white

Cut the margarine into the flour. Blend in egg yolk and sour cream. Knead enough to shape into a ball—the dough is very sticky at this point. Place the bowl into the refrigerator and chill for 2 hours, until firm.

Cut the chilled dough into 3 equal parts. Roll each by hand into a ball. Then, using a rolling pin, roll into a big circle of dough, about 1/8"-1/4" thin. (If the dough is too sticky, add a little more flour.) Once the dough is rolled out, take a knife and cut up the circle into 12 pieces, like a pie. This is easy if you picture a clock face. Leave the pieces where they are.

Blend together all the filling ingredients. (This is best done while the dough is chilling.) Sprinkle some of the filling mixture over the divided circle of dough. Starting at the widest part of each pie-shaped piece, roll the dough (with the filling rolling inside) toward the center, creating a croissant-like shape. Form the shape into a bit of a crescent and place on an ungreased cookie sheet. Glaze with egg-white.

Bake at 375° for 25 minutes or until golden brown.

Mandelbread (a.k.a. Mandelcookies)

1 stick margarine, melted
1/2 cup sugar
3 eggs
1 tsp almond flavoring
3 cup flour
1/2 cup nuts & raisins or 1/2 cup chocolate chips

Mix all the ingredients—the dough will be very sticky. Take a little oil onto your hands and shape the dough into 2 loaves. Place the two loaves onto an ungreased cookie sheet

Bake at 350° for 45 minutes. Cut the loaves into slices about 3/8" wide. Lay the slices flat and put the cookie sheets back into the oven. Brown the slices lightly on each side.

Cholent

This is the dish that you can start on Friday and cook in a low oven or slow-cooking crock pot all day Saturday. It was originally primarily a bean dish that emigrated along with our grandparents from Eastern Europe.

2 cups dried lima beans	1/4 tsp pepper
3 pounds brisket	1/4 tsp ginger
3 onions, diced	1 cup barley
3 tbsp oil	2 tbsp flour
2 tsp salt	2 tsp paprika

Soak the beans overnight in water. Drain in the morning. Use a heavy saucepan or dutch oven and brown the meat and onions in the oil. Sprinkle in salt, pepper, and ginger. Add the beans and barley and sprinkle in the flour and paprika. Add enough boiling water to cover one inch above the ingredients. Cover tightly.

Bake for 24 hours in a 250° oven (for quicker cooking you may cook for 4–5 hours at 350°. You may also use the slow setting on your crock pot. Serves 8–10.

Appendix B
Shabbat Music

Shalom Aleykhem

Gently *Sabbath Liturgy*

Sha-lom A-leykhem, mal-'a-khey ha-sha-a-reyt, mal-'a-khey E- e- e- el

yon. Mi- i- i me-lekh ma-al-khey ham'la-a- khim, ha-ka-dosh ba-rukh

hu. Bo-'a-khem l'-sha-lom, mal-'a-khey ha-sha-a-lom, mal-'a-khe-ey E-el- yon

Mi- i- me-lekh ma-al-khey ham'la-a- khim, ha- ka-a- do-osh ba-a- ru-kh hu.

L'khah Dodi

Moderately *Sabbath Liturgy*

L'— khah do-di li- i- kra't kal-lah p'ney Sha-bbat n'ka-a- b'—

lah. L'— khah do- di li- i- kra't kal- lah p'

ney Sha-bbat n'- ka- a- a- b'- lah. L' khah do- di l'

khah do- di likra't ka-al- lah p'- ney Shab-bat n'- ka ah-b' lah. L'-

khah do-di li- kra't ka- al- lah p' ney Sha-bbat n'- ka-a b' lah.

43

Eliyahu HaNavi

E- li- ya- hu ha- Na- vi, E- li- ya- hu
ha- Tish- bi, E- li- ya- hu E- li- ya- hu
E- li- ya- hu ha- Gi- la- di. Bim- hey- rah ve-
ya- mey- nu ya- vo e- le- ey- nu im Ma- shi- ach
ben Da- vid, im Ma- shi- ach ben Da- vid.

(May the prophet Elijah come soon, in our time, with the Messiah, son of David.)

Behold God Is My Salvation

by Stuart Dauermann
Used by Permission
Integrated Copyright Group

Be- ho- old God is my sal- va- tion I will
trust and will not be a- fraid for the Lord my God is my
strength and my song He al- so has be- come my sal- va- tion for the Lord my God is my
strength and my song He al- so has be- come my sal- va- tion lai-lai lai-lai lai lai lai lai lai
lai- lai- lai lai lai lai lai lai lai lai lai lai lai lai lai lai lai lai lai lai lai

Bibliography

Abbot, Lyman. *Christian Union*. June 26, 1890.

The Artscroll Illustrated Birchon. New York: Mesorah Publications, Ltd., 1996. This booklet contains all the Sabbath prayers and blessings.

Bacchiocchi, Samuele. *From Sabbath to Sunday: A Historical Investigation of the Rise of Sunday Observance in Early Christianity*. Rome: The Pontifical Gregorian University Press, 1977.

Berkowitz, Ariel, and D'vorah Berkowitz. *Shabbat: Celebrating the Sabbath the Messianic Jewish Way*. Baltimore: Lederer Publications, 1991. (Out of Print)

Bloch, Abraham P. *The Biblical and Historical Background of the Jewish Holy Days*. New York: Ktav Publishing House, Inc., 1978.

Dawn, Marva J. *Keeping the Sabbath Wholly: Ceasing, Resting, Embracing, Feasting*. Grand Rapids: Wm. B. Eerdmans Publishing Co., 1989.

Donin, Hayim Halevy. *To Be a Jew*.

Geieman, P. *Convert's Catechism of Catholic Doctrine*.

Fischer, John, and David Bronstein. *Siddur for Messianic Jews*. Palm Harbor, Fla.: Menorah Ministries, 1988. Messianic Jewish Sabbath prayer book. Contains full liturgy.

Gibbons, James Cardinal. *The Faith of Our Fathers*.

Hemenway, Harold. *Which Day is the Sabbath*. 1996.

Heschel, A. J. *The Sabbath: Its Meaning for Modern Man*. New York: Farrar, Straus, and Young, 1951.

Historia Ecclestastica. Edition Basilea, 1624.

Kaplan, Aryeh. *Sabbath: Day of Eternity*, 2nd ed. New York: National Conference of Synagogue Youth, 1984.

Kasdan, Barney. *God's Appointed Times*. Baltimore: Lederer Publications, 1993. Detailed descriptions of the Sabbath and all the biblical holy days.

Millgram, Abraham E. *Sabbath: The Day of Delight*. Philadelphia: JPS, 1947.

National Conference of Synagogue Youth. *The NCSY Bencher: A Book of Prayer and Song*. New York: Union of Orthodox Jewish Congregations, 1983. Contains a complete Orthodox Jewish Sabbath service, including all the prayers, blessings, and songs.

Odom, Robert. *Sabbath and Sunday in Early Christianity*.

Rubin, Steffi. *A Messianic Jewish Art Calendar*. Baltimore: Lederer/Messianic Jewish Publishers, 1998.

Scherman, Nosson. *The Rabbinical Council of America Edition of The Artscroll Siddur*. NY: Mesorah Publications, Ltd., 1990. Orthodox Jewish Sabbath prayer book. Contains full liturgy.

Silverman, Morris. *Sabbath and Festival Prayer Book*. USA: United Synagogue of America, 1979. Conservative Jewish Sabbath and festival prayer book. Contains full liturgy.

Stern, David H. *Complete Jewish Bible* Clarksville, Md.: Jewish New Testament Publications, Inc., 1998. *Tanakh* (Old Testament) plus *B'rit Chadashah*(New Testament) from a Messianic Jewish perspective.

Webb, Levi. *Questions and Answers About the Sabbath*. Chase, Md.: Covenant Ministries, Inc., 1995.